TRISTAN BERNAYS

Tristan Bernays is an award-winning writer and performer from London. His work has been performed at Soho Theatre, Bush Theatre, National Theatre Studio, Roundhouse and Southwark Playhouse. His play *Boudica* was performed at Shakespeare's Globe in September 2017 as part of Emma Rice's Summer of Love season, with Gina McKee in the title role. His show *Teddy* won Best New Musical at the 2016 Off West End Awards, and he was a member of Bush Theatre's Emerging Writers' Group 2016/17. Credits include *Testament* (VAULT Festival; dir: Lucy Jane Atkinson); *Frankenstein* (Watermill Theatre/Wilton's Musical Hall; dir: Eleanor Rhode); *Teddy* (Southwark Playhouse; dir: Eleanor Rhode); *The Bread & The Beer* (Soho Theatre/UK tour; dir: Sophie Larsmon); *Coffin* (King's Head Theatre; dir: Oliver Rose).

Other Titles in this Series

Mike Bartlett
ALBION
BULL
GAME
AN INTERVENTION
KING CHARLES III
WILD

Tristan Bernays
BOUDICA
TESTAMENT

Jez Butterworth
THE FERRYMAN
JERUSALEM
JEZ BUTTERWORTH PLAYS: ONE
MOJO
THE NIGHT HERON
PARLOUR SONG
THE RIVER
THE WINTERLING

Caryl Churchill
BLUE HEART
CHURCHILL PLAYS: THREE
CHURCHILL PLAYS: FOUR
CHURCHILL: SHORTS
CLOUD NINE
DING DONG THE WICKED
A DREAM PLAY *after* Strindberg
DRUNK ENOUGH TO SAY
I LOVE YOU?
ESCAPED ALONE
FAR AWAY
HERE WE GO
HOTEL
ICECREAM
LIGHT SHINING IN
BUCKINGHAMSHIRE
LOVE AND INFORMATION
MAD FOREST
A NUMBER
PIGS AND DOGS
SEVEN JEWISH CHILDREN
THE SKRIKER
THIS IS A CHAIR
THYESTES *after* Seneca
TRAPS

debbie tucker green
BORN BAD
DIRTY BUTTERFLY
HANG
NUT
A PROFOUNDLY AFFECTIONATE,
PASSIONATE DEVOTION TO
SOMEONE (– *NOUN*)
RANDOM
STONING MARY
TRADE & GENERATIONS
TRUTH AND RECONCILIATION

Matt Hartley
DEPOSIT
HERE I BELONG
MICROCOSM
SIXTY FIVE MILES

Sam Holcroft
COCKROACH
DANCING BEARS
EDGAR & ANNABEL
PINK
RULES FOR LIVING
THE WARDROBE
WHILE YOU LIE

Vicky Jones
THE ONE
TOUCH

Anna Jordan
CHICKEN SHOP
FREAK
YEN

Andrew Keatley
ALLIGATORS
THE GATHERED LEAVES

Lucy Kirkwood
BEAUTY AND THE BEAST
with Katie Mitchell
BLOODY WIMMIN
THE CHILDREN
CHIMERICA
HEDDA *after* Ibsen
IT FELT EMPTY WHEN THE HEART
WENT AT FIRST BUT IT IS
ALRIGHT NOW
LUCY KIRKWOOD PLAYS: ONE
MOSQUITOES
NSFW
TINDERBOX

Sam Potter
HANNA

Katherine Soper
WISH LIST

Jack Thorne
2ND MAY 1997
A CHRISTMAS CAROL *after* Dickens
BUNNY
BURYING YOUR BROTHER
IN THE PAVEMENT
HOPE
JACK THORNE PLAYS: ONE
JUNKYARD
LET THE RIGHT ONE IN
after John Ajvide Lindqvist
MYDIDAE
STACY & FANNY AND FAGGOT
WHEN YOU CURE ME
WOYZECK *after* Büchner

Phoebe Waller-Bridge
FLEABAG

Tom Wells
BROKEN BISCUITS
FOLK
JUMPERS FOR GOALPOSTS
THE KITCHEN SINK
ME, AS A PENGUIN

Tristan Bernays

OLD FOOLS

NICK HERN BOOKS
London
www.nickhernbooks.co.uk

A Nick Hern Book

Old Fools first published in Great Britain as a paperback original in 2018 by Nick Hern Books Limited, The Glasshouse, 49a Goldhawk Road, London W12 8QP, in association with To the Moon and Making Productions

Cover image: Francesca Tortora

Designed and typeset by Nick Hern Books, London
Printed in the UK by Mimeo Ltd, Huntingdon, Cambridgeshire PE29 6XX

A CIP catalogue record for this book is available from the British Library

ISBN 978 1 84842 748 8

Woodland CARBON
www.woodlandcarbon.co.uk
NICK HERN BOOKS
Printed on Carbon Captured paper

Old Fools was first performed at Southwark Playhouse, London, on 14 March 2018, with the following cast:

TOM	Mark Arends
VIV	Frances Grey
Director	Sharon Burrell
Movement Director	Lucie Pankhurst
Lighting Designer	Peter Small
Sound Designer / Composer	Christopher Ash
Sound Designer	Patrick Ball
Costume	Anto Cossu
Assistant Director	Samuel Quested
Deputy Stage Manager	Remi Bruno Smith
Casting Director	Sophie Parrott
Producer	Sharon Burrell
Producer	Darren Murphy
General Manager	Julie Clare
Press	Kevin Wilson
Digital Marketing	Rob Landi

OLD FOOLS

Tristan Bernays

‘I urge you to please notice when you are happy,
and exclaim or murmur or think at some point:
“If this isn’t nice, I don’t know what is.”’

Kurt Vonnegut

Acknowledgements

I wrote *Old Fools* four years ago and spent two years unsuccessfully trying to get it produced. Eventually, I had to admit defeat and condemn the play to the back of a drawer, never to be seen again.

Then two weeks later, Sharon asked if she could produce and direct it. Which goes to show that (a) you never know what the future will hold and (b) nothing is ever wasted.

I'd like to thank the following for helping to get *Old Fools* from page to stage:

Sharon Burrell, Darren Murphy and everyone at To The Moon and Making Productions.

The cast, creative and technical team.

Sophie Parrott for her casting expertise.

All the staff at Southwark Playhouse – from Production to Front of House and Box Office.

All the actors, directors and anyone else who helped workshop and develop the show over the years.

Champ (she's good police).

My family (for the inspiration).

You (for watching my plays and reading my scripts).

T.B.
March 2018

This play is dedicated to my grandparents:

Freda Joan Keneally Ainsworth O'Farrell – Nana
Patrick Vincent O'Farrell – Grandpa
Diana Marie Lang Bernays – Grandma
Frederic George Bernays – Grandpa

And also to William Houston Rowe – Uncle Bill

Characters

TOM
VIV

Note

The play seamlessly slides through memories, times and places.

In each memory, the characters are somewhere else, some time else and even someone else.

The actor playing Tom plays him at various stages of his life.

The actor playing Viv plays her at various stages of her life, as well as other characters from Tom's life.

Shifts in time, place and character are marked in the text in bold.

It is at the discretion of the creative team how they shift between memories.

Consider them like cuts in a film: some of them are jump-cuts, some of them are wipes, some of them are fades.

The shifts should not be obviously marked out for an audience. They should be fluid and seamless, like thoughts.

This text went to press before the end of rehearsals and so may differ slightly from the play as performed.

TOM. I saw that.

VIV. What?

TOM. Just then.

VIV. What?

TOM. Winking.

VIV. Winking?

TOM. You didn't wink at me?

VIV. No.

TOM. Must have been your eye then.

VIV. My eye?

TOM. Of its own accord.

VIV. How do you know it wasn't just an eyelash?

TOM. Oh no, not that wink.

VIV. No?

TOM. No no. I happen to be an expert on lovely eyes and the winks they make.

VIV. That wink could have been anything. An eyelash. Or a mote of dust.

TOM. Oh no, that wink was saying something alright.

VIV. Which is what?

TOM. I couldn't possibly say.

VIV. Why not?

TOM. Because that's a secret between me and your Lovely Blue Eye. I couldn't possibly betray that confidence with a stranger.

VIV. A stranger?

TOM. I hardly know you.

VIV. And yet you're on first name terms with my eye?

TOM. In fairness it did make the first move.

VIV. I must have a word with it for being so forward.

TOM. Don't take it out on such a pretty eye.

VIV. I will do just that. In fact, if it persists in betraying my confidence to handsome young men, I will take it right out of my head.

TOM. You'd cut off your nose to spite your face?

VIV. Now my nose is getting in on the action? Pretty soon all of my face will be rebelling and going off to do its own business. I'll have my eyes by my elbows and my ears round my knees and my lips will be off gallivanting round with who knows what.

TOM. You'll be a Picasso. They'll hang you in the Louvre. Though I've got an empty space at my place that needs filling.

VIV. So you can ogle me nightly? No thank you.

TOM. You were ogling me.

VIV. Was not.

TOM. Were too. Your eye –

VIV. Ah yes, my eye again. You seem rather taken with my eye.

TOM. Don't be jealous. I am rather taken with the rest of you too. You're not like the others.

VIV. No?

TOM. People come here to make a fuss and be seen. And there's an awful lot of folks in here making an awful lot of noise.

VIV. I think the man at the piano was making the most.

TOM. I'll let you have that since you were so nice to me before.

VIV. When was that?

TOM. Just now. You called me handsome.

VIV. I did no such thing.

TOM. You did.

VIV. You must have misheard.

TOM. I never mishear. I have excellent hearing.

VIV. You must have misremembered.

TOM. I never misremember. I'm like an elephant – never forget.

VIV. Well I would never say such a thing – even if it were true.

TOM. Are you saying it isn't?

VIV. Well I can't deny there is perhaps – some handsomeness to you.

TOM. Some handsomeness?

VIV. In a certain light.

TOM. Apology accepted.

VIV. I didn't apologise.

TOM. Well then you owe me something.

VIV. What?

TOM. A dance.

VIV. I'm not so sure.

TOM. Afraid your date will get jealous?

VIV. What date?

TOM. Man in the blue suit.

VIV. He's not a date.

TOM. Then what's the harm in a dance?

VIV. …

TOM. I love this song.

VIV. Fred and Ginger.

TOM. Now he was a dancer.

VIV. Not as good as Ginger.

TOM. What?

VIV. Ginger did everything that Fred did but backwards and in heels.

TOM. But Ginger couldn't sing like Fred could.

TOM *sings the first verse of 'The Way You Look Tonight' by Dorothy Fields and Jerome Kern.*

VIV. You sing –

TOM. Yes?

VIV. – beautifully.

TOM. Thank you. You dance –

VIV. Yes?

TOM. – beautifully.

VIV. Thank you.

TOM. Tom.

VIV. Vivian.

TOM. Does your date know you dance so well?

VIV. He's not a date, I told you.

TOM. I'm not sure you told him.

VIV. He's a friend from the office.

TOM. Very friendly it seems. Hasn't let you buy a drink all night.

VIV. You keeping tab? You should be concentrating on playing.

TOM. I can do two things at once. I'm very adept at multitasking. For example, while I am dancing an exemplary foxtrot with you –

VIV. Sloppy.

TOM. What?

VIV. Not exemplary – sloppy.

TOM. Sloppy? You're calling my dancing sloppy?

VIV. But not without its charm.

TOM. I'll have you know girls have lined up round the block to dance with me.

VIV. Good thing too – you need the practice.

TOM. Well since you're the expert how about a couple of pointers my way?

VIV. Alright. Loosen your legs. Straighten your back. Relax your shoulders. And hold me like you mean it. Strong but light. You can't force a dance out of me – you have to coax it.

Okay?

One step, two step. One step, two step.

TOM. One step –

VIV. – two step.

TOM. Legs loose –

VIV. – but strong. Back straight –

TOM. – nice and long.

VIV. Ready for a turn?

TOM. Always.

VIV. Lift the arm.

TOM. Palm –

VIV. – and turn.

TOM. Easy.

VIV. Isn't it?

TOM. How about a dip?

VIV. Oh!

TOM. You alright?

VIV. Yes.

TOM. I'm a fast learner.

VIV. I can see.

TOM. Ready for a grand finale?

VIV. Alright.

TOM. Lift the arm, palm and turn and lift the arm and palm and turn and –

VIV. **Lift the arm up.** Up, up. That's it. Scrub along there. And your pits. Other arm. Give us your fingers. Got to get under the nails. Get all the black out. Okay, lift your – lift your – thing. That's it. Don't want you getting dirty there, do we? And the feet. Scrub them nice and – Nails are getting long. Must do your – There. Like a new pin.

Doesn't that feel good?

TOM. …

You forgot behind the ears.

VIV. I didn't.

TOM. Scrub behind your ears, else you'll get potatoes growing there.

VIV. I won't.

TOM. You will. I can already see a couple sprouting. We'll have to chop them up and turn them into chips.

VIV. Fish and chips!

TOM. And mushy peas.

VIV. Peas in the bath?

TOM. When I was a lad, I was the youngest of nine and always the last in the bath – a tin bath that we had in front of the fire. And by the time I got in, the water was always higher than when it started and still warm. You know why?

VIV. Why?

TOM. Peas in the bath. Psssssss.

VIV. No!

TOM. Yes.

VIV. Errr!

TOM. Errr!

VIV. Mommy says you're a fibber.

TOM. Does she?

VIV. Says you make up stories.

TOM. What do you think?

VIV. Where do babies come from?

TOM. You buy them from the shops.

VIV. See!

TOM. What?

VIV. You're a fibber!

TOM. Am not.

VIV. Are too!

TOM. Am not! You buy them from the shops – aisle six, next to the milk. We got you half-price cos they were having a sale that day.

VIV. Daddy!

TOM. Look, you wouldn't believe me if I told you, Alice.

VIV. Tell me!

TOM. Alright.

VIV. Tell me!

TOM. Alright! Before you were born, before there was even a little baby Alice, you were a – a little tadpole and a little egg.

VIV. An egg?

TOM. Yes, an egg. Like that. And the tadpole swam up to the egg like that and they did a – little dance thing and then – poof! You were a baby.

VIV. You're fibbing!

TOM. I'm not!

VIV. Yes, you are!

TOM. I'm not, I swear I'm not – that's how you were born. Like that. Well, not just like that, you – You can't imagine what – You, Alice, were a particularly fragile egg, very nearly didn't – but that's what makes you so special. Why Mummy and I are so lucky to have you.

VIV. Billy Prissop at school says that a boy puts a baby in your tummy and then it comes out of your mummy's cuckoo.

TOM. Does he?

VIV. But if babies are so big how do they get up there?

TOM. I think Billy Prissop needs to wash his mouth out with soap and water. And you need to get ready for bed.

VIV. No.

TOM. Now come on.

VIV. I don't wanna.

TOM. We've been over this. I'm not doing this again.

VIV. No.

TOM. You're going to sleep whether you want to or not.

VIV. Can't make me.

TOM. I can.

VIV. Can't!

TOM. Can!

VIV. Can't!

TOM. Can!

VIV. Can't!

TOM. Can!

VIV. Can't!

TOM. **Can't**!

VIV. Can!

TOM. Can't!

VIV. Can!

TOM. Can't!

VIV. Can!

TOM. Can't can't can't!

VIV. Can can can can!

TOM. Aaaaah!

VIV. Tom!

TOM. Aaaaah!

VIV. Tom please, for the love of God, just –

TOM. No!

VIV. Just lie down, please, and –

TOM. No!

VIV. – go to sleep.

TOM. Bitch!

VIV. Not tonight, Tom, please I –

TOM. Just let me – l-l-l-leave me to –

VIV. – haven't got the strength tonight, Tom, to –

TOM. Just fuck off and –

VIV. Don't talk to me like that, Tom, don't talk to me like – I am just –

TOM. Fuck off, you stupid –

VIV. Tom, I –

TOM. Fuck off!

VIV. Fine, fine, you want me to – to – I'll just go then, Tom, I'll just –

TOM. **What?**

VIV. I'm going.

TOM. No.

VIV. Yes.

TOM. Why?

VIV. I'm sorry, I have to go.

TOM. No, you don't.

VIV. Yes, I do.

TOM. What possible reason could you have to leave this bed?

VIV. You are making this very hard –

TOM. Because you want to stay. Don't you?

VIV. …

TOM. Aha!

VIV. Have you seen the time?

TOM. Clock's wrong. Never wind it. Runs fast.

VIV. The sun's up.

TOM. That's the moon.

VIV. Tom –

TOM. Good God – she's hysterical, delirious! Nurse, quick!

VIV. I have to get ready!

TOM. I can't in all good conscience allow you outside. As a medical professional I insist you stay here and let me tend to you.

VIV. And what would that involve exactly?

TOM. Let me show you.

VIV. No, no, no – D'you want me to get this job or not?

TOM. Of course.

VIV. Then let me go study.

TOM. You want I should help you revise?

VIV. How's your knowledge of modern French economics and Anglo-Franco relations?

TOM. Terrible – but I can order a coffee with great success.

VIV. If it wasn't for me you'd've starved to death by now.

TOM. *Bonjour, mademoiselle, un café s'il vous plaît.*

VIV. Oh, you've been practising. Very good.

TOM. *Juste un peu.*

VIV. Super. *Qu'est ce que tu peux dire de plus?*

TOM. *Oh, beaucoup, beaucoup. Er... Excusez-moi, monsieur, est-ce qu'il y a un bibliothèque proche?*

VIV. *Bien sûr! C'est tout droit, là bas.*

TOM. *Et la plage?*

VIV. *À gauche.*

TOM. *Voulez-vous venir avec moi?*

VIV. *Oh, monsieur, vous êtes très méchant – je sais que la seule raison pour laquelle vous avez demandé la direction de la plage d'une jolie femme comme moi, c'est que vous avez des mauvaises intentions. Ça-va ça-vient, uh?*

TOM. . . .

What?

VIV. *Alors, je peux être une souris, mais ça ne signifie pas que vous pouvez voir ma chatte.*

TOM. I don't – What are you – ?

VIV. *Parant son tien, boutou vou voulant pour ça?*

TOM. I don't – Viv, I don't –

VIV. *Et courant pouto fondrillé.*

TOM. Viv, you're not – You don't don't don't – d-d-d don't – don't –

VIV. Nours attattant fatifafa eh? Eh?

TOM. I d-d-d-die die – die – I –

VIV. **Tom? Cantou telma quoi es, Tom?**

TOM. I p-p-p – would – would –

VIV. Tom?

Can you tell me what that is?

TOM. It's – er – it's a tree.

VIV. Good. And this one?

TOM. A chair.

VIV. And this?

Erm – that's a – erm –

That's a – p – p-p-p – oh, it's a – it's a – Oh, one those – things you play with the – keys – it's er –

Piano.

VIV. **Full time?**

TOM. Yeah.

VIV. Are you serious? Tom, that's –

TOM. I know, yeah –

VIV. That's just – What did they say?

TOM. Said they liked the way I played. Wanted me to keep me on for the record.

VIV. Record? They're doing a –

TOM. Yeah.

VIV. Oh my God, Tom, that's –

TOM. I know –

VIV. That's amazing!

TOM. I know, but –

VIV. What did you say?

TOM. I said I'd think about it.

VIV. What?

TOM. I said I'd –

VIV. What? What are you talking about?

TOM. It's in Rome, Viv.

VIV. Rome?

TOM. Marco knows this fella from Black Saint over in Rome, they do all the avant-garde stuff all the – Archie Shepp, that kind of – And they've got this new label Soul Note, it's more mainstream, more our kind of thing and – And he came over a couple of weeks back, liked what he saw and he says that he wants to get them in the studio.

VIV. When?

TOM. Soon as he can.

VIV. And would he – I mean would you go out there just for the recording?

TOM. He wants us there for that, yeah, but – He's got this whole series of gigs lined up for us.

VIV. How many?

TOM. I don't know but – He wants to launch us in Rome, you know. Make us part of the scene out there.

VIV. So how long would it be?

TOM. Well it would – It'd be a permanent thing. The whole band's moving out there.

VIV. For good?

TOM. Yeah.

VIV. When does Marco need to know?

TOM. Friday. They got a guy they were gonna go with but Marco said they liked playing with me the last few weeks. Wanted to ask me first before they go with this other fella.

I said I'd think about it, talk to you but –

VIV. What?

TOM. I can tell you're not –

VIV. No, no it's not that, I'm not –

TOM. And that's fine, of course, I'm not –

VIV. It's just –

TOM. I'm totally fine with that, I –

VIV. – a lot to take in, I just have to work out – Think how we'd –

TOM. I don't wanna uproot the whole family –

VIV. You're not –

TOM. You know, work's going so well for you – Alice starting school, I –

VIV. Tom, this is big.

TOM. I know but –

VIV. I mean what else have you been putting all this work in for if you don't –

TOM. I don't wanna fuck things up.

VIV. What?

TOM. Everything. This – that. Rome and here, I don't –

VIV. Who says it's going to – You haven't even got there yet.

TOM. But what if it does?

VIV. Then we'll deal with it. Together, all of us. You and me and us and Alice.

TOM. I don't know if we can do it, Viv, I don't know if I could –

VIV. What happens if you don't do it?

TOM. Well – Nothing, I –

VIV. And if you do? You're brilliant, Tom, and if you don't just take a risk and do this you'll be kicking yourself for the rest of your life.

Now tell me, honestly – do you want do it?

TOM. …

Yeah.

VIV. Well that's it then, isn't it? We're doing it.

TOM. You mean it?

VIV. I mean it.

TOM. Yeah?

VIV. Yeah.

TOM. Well – Alright.

VIV. Alright?

TOM. Alright, yeah. Yeah. Yeah, we're doing this.

VIV. We're doing this.

TOM. We're doing this, we're fucking doing – I love you.

VIV. I love you.

TOM. Oh my God, we're doing this, we're – Get your bags packed, Viv, get your tickets cos we are leaving, we are getting on that plane!

VIV. **Oh God.**

TOM. What?

VIV. Oh God, where the hell did I –

TOM. What?

VIV. I had them – Here! I had them right here, I put them them right there with the passports when we went through security and now they're not –

TOM. What?

VIV. The tickets! What d'you think –

TOM. Alright. Don't get crabby with me or I won't tell you where they are.

VIV. What? Where are they?

TOM. I told you, I won't tell you if –

VIV. Tom, please, where are th–

TOM. Front pocket.

VIV. …

TOM. See?

VIV. Jesus.

TOM. We're fine.

VIV. I –

TOM. No need to –

VIV. Where's Alice?

TOM. She's over there.

VIV. Alice!

TOM. Viv –

VIV. Alice, stay where I can see you, darling.

TOM. She's fine.

VIV. Stay where Mummy can –

TOM. Would you leave her be? She's not going anywhere. You couldn't smuggle a pack of fags up your arse in here, you really think someone's going to run off with her?

VIV. I just want to make sure she's okay.

TOM. Are you – Are you nervous?

VIV. What?

TOM. Are you nervous? I'm the one who's supposed to be –

VIV. Course I'm – flipping nervous!

TOM. Six languages and you can't swear in any of them.

VIV. I've got to –

TOM. I don't think I've ever actually seen you nervous.

VIV. I am trying to think about what I've got to prepare –

TOM. And I am trying to take your mind off it.

VIV. What if I forget?

TOM. What?

VIV. Everything!

TOM. Oh, come on.

VIV. I keep having this dream that we're in Rome and I'm at the consulate and I have to introduce all these diplomats and people and I – I'm supposed to start translating but then they start talking and I have no idea what they're saying and I have to start making up gobbledygook Italian on the spot.

TOM. Least you weren't naked in it.

VIV. Small mercies.

TOM. I'm always naked in mine. Playing away without a stitch on. Funny thing is, I always seem to get a bigger applause than usual.

VIV. Shouldn't we be boarding now or something?

TOM. Viv –

VIV. I mean, we've been waiting here for more than – We – Shouldn't we ask someone if –

TOM. Would you just relax?

VIV. What if it's not –

TOM. You are going to be great. They wouldn't have offered you the job if they didn't think so. You are going to be great. We are going to be great.

Okay?

VIV. Okay.

TOM. Okay. So say goodbye to Barcelona and hello to Roma! A new start, eh? Gonna be great. Gonna be exciting, isn't it? Isn't it?

VIV. Yes. Yes it is.

TOM. Exactly – it's going to be great.

Besides if it all falls through you can hold my hat while I busk.

VIV. What?

TOM. I'll play romantic ballads by the Trevi Fountain for love-twined tourists and you can jangle the change in my hat.

VIV. Lire don't jangle.

TOM. You can rustle the change in my hat and turn the sheet music for me.

VIV. You've another thing coming if you think I'm going to be your page-turner all my life.

TOM. I have an excellent pension scheme.

VIV. Oh no. You think I'm going to be able to afford a seaside apartment in Sitges with the pennies you toss me –

TOM. Lire.

VIV. Lire – with the lire you toss me from busking?

TOM. Sitges?

VIV. Mmm-hmm.

TOM. Oh yes of course – you and Jörgen in your little place by the sea.

VIV. Do you think we'll be okay?

TOM. Oh yes, I'm sure the two of you will be very happy.

VIV. Tom.

TOM. And I do hope that you'll still be wearing that little two-piece.

VIV. Tom.

TOM. What?

VIV. I'm serious, I'm not –

TOM. Viv – I don't doubt it for a second

And you did look dynamite in that two-piece.

VIV. Did?

TOM. Do – not did.

VIV. Did?

TOM. Do. I definitely mean do.

VIV. I can't believe –

TOM. I'm joking.

VIV. No.

TOM. Come here.

VIV. No.

TOM. Come here.

VIV. No, no – No, Tom, no!

TOM. What?

VIV. Get off!

TOM. What? I'm not doing –

VIV. Tom, I mean it!

TOM. I thought you'd like a cuddle!

VIV. You're soaking!

TOM. Okay, okay. You should have come in – water's lovely and cool.

VIV. Yes – I can feel that, thank you. I was just enjoying the sun then.

TOM. Oh, I'm sorry.

VIV. No you're not.

TOM. You should have come and had a roll about in the surf.

VIV. Like *From Here To Eternity*?

TOM. Mmmm.

VIV. That make you Burt Lancaster?

TOM. Your words, not mine.

VIV. You wish.

TOM. I could see you watching.

VIV. What?

TOM. Oh yeah – I saw you having a sneaky peek.

VIV. I don't know what you're talking about.

TOM. You weren't watching me?

VIV. Maybe. You did look rather nice coming out the water.

TOM. Like Burt Lanc–

VIV. Like Burt Lancaster, yes.

TOM. You don't look too bad yourself in that two-piece. Mmmm.

VIV. Hey, you're still dripping on me.

TOM. All lovely and brown like melted butter.

VIV. I feel like melted butter.

TOM. You taste like it too.

VIV. Can we just stay here forever?

TOM. I don't see why not. We could live on the beach and eat fish straight out the sea.

VIV. Oh no. No, I'd need a proper place. Little seaside apartment.

TOM. Well, that may be some time coming on what I earn.

VIV. But when you make it big.

TOM. Well.

VIV. Gonna come back here with a little nest egg. Get me a little place by the sea, just on the beach. Get me a toy boy and sit on my balcony and watch him do laps in the ocean.

TOM. A toy boy.

VIV. Jörgen.

TOM. Jörgen?

VIV. Swedish gymnast. Terribly nice. Doesn't speak a word of English.

TOM. And where do I fit into this?

VIV. Oh you're long gone by this point.

TOM. Am I?

VIV. It was very sad.

TOM. Was it?

VIV. Freak piano accident. You hit a high-C and the wire snapped and took your head clean off.

TOM. Took it off?

VIV. I wore black for a whole year.

TOM. How thoughtful of you.

VIV. Oh, I could just melt. Lie here all day and just melt and then wash away with the tide out to sea.

TOM. I'd come and rescue you.

VIV. Would you?

TOM. I would. Scoop you up and bring you back here all safe and sound.

VIV. How sweet.

TOM. Would Jörgen do that for you?

VIV. Probably not. Tell the truth, he probably wouldn't look as nice coming out the water either, like – like – **Oh what's his name.** That fella from the movies. You know. What's his name? The one with – When they were kissing in the sea, in the surf, during the war.

Frank Sinatra was in it. They were kissing in the sea.

Not like this, I mean. Bit nippy for swimming with your sweetheart in this but – Well, maybe we could have a dip, eh? Don't even need our bathing suits, we could just go – Skinny dip. Might be a shock to the system. Not as much as the shock for that lot up there though. What you reckon, Tom? Shall we give all those old buggers up there something to talk about? I mean we can hardly talk with our – Pair of wrinkly old bums bobbing around in the sea.

Not exactly a little place in Sitges by the sea but it's beautiful, isn't it, Tom? Eh?

If this isn't nice, I don't know what is.

Alice and Russell are going to meet us back at the hotel. The boys'll be there too. They'll be pleased to see you. Have some lunch with them.

Getting a bit cold now, isn't it? Sun's going in. Bit blustery. Feel like I'm being blown about.

Hey – what do you say that we get something before lunch? How about an ice cream? Eh? Would you like an ice cream?

Shall we get an ice cream?

Russell'd say it'll spoil our appetite but – fuck it.

TOM....

Fuck it.

VIV....

Fuck it.

TOM. Fuck it!

VIV. Fuck it!

TOM *and* VIV. Fuck it! Fuck fuck fuck it!

...

VIV. I love you, you silly old sod.

TOM. I love you.

VIV....

TOM. I love you.

VIV. I love you too.

TOM. I love you, Mummy.

VIV....

I'm not your mummy.

TOM. I love –

VIV. I'm not your mummy.

TOM. **Hey.**

VIV. I'm not going to be anyone's mummy.

TOM. Hey, hey it's –

VIV. I'm not going to be anyone's mummy.

TOM. Shhh shhh shhh, hey it's okay. It's okay, come here. It's okay.

VIV. What if I can't?

TOM. Stop it.

VIV. What if I can't –

TOM. Stop that, you hear? Don't be – It's not your fault. It's not anyone's fault. It is what it is.

VIV. What if – what if I'm not supposed to –

TOM. Don't you say that. Don't you dare. You'll be a mummy. A beautiful mummy with a beautiful baby girl in your arms.

VIV. A girl?

TOM. A girl.

VIV. How do you figure that?

TOM. I've got a hunch. A beautiful baby girl. And before that you'll get all round and big-bellied –

VIV. Okay.

TOM. A big round belly, all glowing.

VIV. Stop it!

TOM. Like a cow.

VIV. Okay, stop it!

TOM. And I'll love you just the same. Round and beautiful as you are. I'll love you and I'll love that little thing when she comes out. You'll be the best fucking mummy in the whole wide world.

VIV. In the whole wide world.

TOM. The whole wide world we'll go, the three of us. I mean, why do we have to stick around in Paris? We don't have to – We've got the whole world at our fingertips. We can go anywhere we want. Where d'you wanna go?

VIV. I don't – I don't –

TOM. Come on, Viv, where d'you wanna go? Where d'you wanna go? Anywhere.

VIV. Barcelona.

TOM. Barcelona! There you go –

VIV. I've always wanted to go there.

TOM. Barcelona, we can to go to Barcelona! Or Rome, we could go to Rome. Or Brussels. Or Bruges. Or Bucharest –

VIV. Or Berlin!

TOM. Berlin, exactly! Berlin, they got a great music scene there – I know a guy who – Or Monte Carlo. Or Madrid. Or Vienna. Or Amsterdam. Or Lisbon.

VIV. **Reading.**

TOM. Reading?

VIV. Yes, Reading. They've offered me a position there. At the university.

TOM. Why?

VIV. Well, cos I'm bloody qualified –

TOM. No, no I don't mean that, I mean – I mean why Reading?

VIV. Well – why not? It's a good job, the pay is way above what I'm on now, it's security and – I miss home.

TOM. This – This is home. You and me and us and Alice.

VIV. I want her to have a real home, I don't want to keep dragging her all over the world. It's not fair.

TOM. Are you kidding? Most kids would dream of – She'll have all the languages and –

VIV. And what about you? What are you going to do for work?

TOM. I'm playing. I'll keep playing and we'll work on the album and –

VIV. We need something more secure.

TOM. Secure.

VIV. I spoke to Jenny. She says that they're looking for a teacher.

TOM. No.

VIV. Peripatetic.

TOM. I am not –

VIV. It's good money and regular, and there's still time –

TOM. We can get by fine –

VIV. I can't support all of us –

TOM. I'm not asking you to.

VIV. – on what I'm earning now.

TOM. So what, I have to – go back to scales and finger exercises for pudgy little –

VIV. No, Tom, I'm not – I just can't do this any more. On my own, I – I need someone who's going to be here with me –

TOM. I am here with you, Viv, I'm standing right here –

VIV. I mean right here right now, not – Not just someone I see passing through the door when we – You always say, 'Oh, it's you and me and us and Alice' but you're always – I mean this album –

TOM. Oh, don't –

VIV. When is it actually –

TOM. What, you think it just gonna happen overnight, you – You have to be patient –

VIV. I have been patient, Tom, I have been infinitely fucking patient, and meanwhile Alice is growing up and our life is flying by –

TOM. So, what I have to just – jack it all in and bury myself in a semi-detached in the middle of fucking Reading? Why have I got to give it all up? Why do I –

VIV. Because my work supports us, Tom. My work feeds us and clothes us and puts food on the table. My work is actually worth something. What's yours worth?

TOM. . . .

. . .

. . .

VIV. Tom.

Tom, where are you going? Where are you going?

TOM. Out.

VIV. Well, goodnight!

TOM. Goodnight!

VIV. **Goodnight.**

TOM. Goodnight.

VIV. I had – a charming time.

TOM. A charming time?

VIV. Yes.

TOM. Well – I'm glad. I had a charming time too.

VIV. Good.

TOM. Good.

. . .

Goodnight.

VIV. Goodnight.

TOM. I'm playing again. This Saturday. A place called the Basement or something, le – Le Sous – Sous – Soupçon or something –

VIV. Le Sous-Sol?

TOM. I'm playing with my regular band, we – We're pretty tight.

VIV. Are you?

TOM. Could be pretty big.

You should come along and watch. You could bring your date.

VIV. He was not a date.

TOM. Either way I never got a chance to thank him for introducing us.

I'd love it if you came along to watch. Maybe I could call you and –

VIV. Will there be dancing?

TOM. Oh yes.

VIV....

I'm thirty-two seventeen forty-two ninety-three.

TOM. That your number or your measurements?

VIV. Careful.

TOM. I'll call you.

VIV. Call me what?

TOM. Beautiful.

VIV....

See you later.

TOM....

32 17 42 93.

32 17 42 –

32 17 42 90 –

90 –

90 – something.

VIV. 100 minus 7.

TOM. I know, I know, don't – don't – Sorry don't –

VIV. It's okay.

TOM. It's 90 something, I don't know why I can't –

VIV. Okay. Okay. Let's try something else. Earlier, I showed you three pictures. Three objects. Can you tell me what they were?

TOM. They were – um – They were –

Tree.

Chair.

Chair.

Chair – um –

VIV. Okay.

TOM. Oh Christ, this is so –

VIV. It's okay.

TOM. This is so bloody – stupid, it's –

VIV. There's no need to feel –

TOM. I'm not.

VIV. Okay.

TOM. I'm not embarrassed.

VIV. Okay, let's move –

TOM. I'm not – embarrassed, you're the one who's –

VIV. Okay.

TOM. **You're embarrassed!**

VIV. I'm not.

TOM. Yes, you are!

VIV. Dad, shut up, I am not –

TOM. Alice, you're embarrassed!

VIV. I cannot believe this, I –

TOM. You don't want anyone to see me, do you?

VIV. No, I –

TOM. Am I that uncool? I can be hip.

VIV. Who says hip? Nobody says hip!

TOM. Come on – Cowabunga!

VIV. Oh my God, I am going to kill you –

TOM. Do the Hustle! Doot doot doot da-doot da-doot doot doot –

VIV. I am going to strangle you.

TOM. What, cos I'm so funky?

VIV. Oh my God!

TOM. Come on, let me give you a lift. I promise I won't embarrass you in front of your new cool uni friends – all wearing berets with a copy of Sartre sticking out their back pockets.

VIV. No one's reading Sartre!

TOM. Oh no, no of course, stupid of me – too mainstream. So who is the cool existentialist philosopher-of-choice for you young people these days?

VIV. Oh my God, I swear I'll come back end of term and Mum will have murdered you, you're so –

TOM. I'm hoping she's going to stuff and mount me. I'd make a jolly good Chesterfield. Come on, let me give you a lift.

VIV. Dad, I'm happy making my own way.

TOM. I know you are but I won't see you till the end of term.

VIV. It's a four-hour round trip.

TOM. It's Sunday, Mum's away, I have literally nothing to do. Come on. Humour me.

VIV. I can't.

TOM. Why not?

VIV. Because – I'm already getting a lift.

TOM. Oh. Right. Okay.

From whom?

VIV. A friend.

TOM. Would this friend's name happen to be Russell?

VIV. How do you –

TOM. I have my spies.

VIV. Oh my God, she told you!

TOM. She –

VIV. She fucking told – I can't believe she told you!

TOM. She didn't – but that doesn't mean I didn't overhear you.

VIV. You were listening?

TOM. It's a little difficult not to when you two are cackling and gossiping at full volume. So what's he like?

VIV. He's – nice.

TOM. Nice?

VIV. Yes, nice. What do you want?

TOM. Anything else other than nice?

VIV. He's – kind and considerate and he's – nice.

TOM. And what does Nice-Boy Russell do exactly?

VIV. He does computing.

TOM. Oh, he's one of those, is he?

VIV. Stop it!

TOM. What?

VIV. You always fucking do this! Make fun of my –

TOM. I'm only joking!

VIV. This is why I don't –

TOM. I'm joking, alright? I'm only joking. Come on, give us a smile.

That's better. You look beautiful when you smile. You've got your mother's smile.

VIV. Yeah? What I get from you?

TOM. My foul mouth. And my good looks.

VIV. Fuck off.

TOM. You fuck off. You got her eyes though.

VIV. Yeah?

TOM. Definitely. Those same lovely blue eyes. Hope Nice-Boy likes them.

VIV. **Don't!**

TOM. What? What did I do?

VIV. You know what you did.

TOM. But he is nice. He's super nice. That's why we call him Nice-Boy.

VIV. We do not call him anything – you call him that.

TOM. I heard you call him that just the other day.

VIV. I don't know what you mean.

TOM. You did, I heard you. You called him Nice-Boy –

VIV. You know she doesn't like it when you call him that.

TOM. Then what am I supposed to call him?

VIV. How about Russell?

TOM. Makes him sound like a pile of leaves.

VIV. She wants to bring him over at Christmas.

TOM. Does she?

VIV. I said we'd be thrilled to have him.

TOM. Did you?

VIV. It's going to be his first Christmas away from home – he went back home to the States for Thanksgiving but – So I thought he'd be a little less homesick if he was with us.

TOM. Does that mean I'm going to have to get him a Christmas present?

VIV. Probably. Tom, where's the wine?

TOM. I wouldn't know where to start with a present for him.

VIV. Wine's always good. Speaking of which –

TOM. I tell you, I won't get him one if he keeps talking to me about RAM and giggly-bytes or whatever the hell it is he does. Told me last time about computers that make music like Mozart.

VIV. He's just trying to find a common ground.

TOM. Play it too.

VIV. Tom, where is it?

TOM. Said I wouldn't be getting one.

VIV. Tom!

TOM. What?

VIV. The wine.

TOM. I put it in the – in the –

I put it in the –

…

VIV. Tom?

TOM. …

Sorry, love, my – stupid of me, I, erm – erm – must have put it down when I was –

When I was –

VIV. When you were what, Tom? Love? When you were what?

Tom?

Yoo-hoo!

Tom?

Tom?

TOM. …

I'll pick it up when I –

VIV. Tom?

TOM. Yes, love?

VIV. Where were you?

TOM. When?

VIV. Just now. You –

TOM. What?

VIV. – just sort of – stopped for a moment and then –

TOM. Did I?

VIV. Yes.

TOM. Well I – I – I don't know, I must've been – Sorry, not really thinking today, my brain's all –

VIV. You okay?

TOM. Yeah, yeah, fine.

VIV. You sure?

TOM. Right as rain. Honest.

VIV. Well – okay. If you're –

TOM. Yeah, course I am, love, I – Listen I'll pick up a bottle on the way back from the station, yeah?

VIV. Well, you better be going – Alice and Nice-Boy'll be here soon.

TOM. Aha!

VIV. What?

TOM. You did it. You just did it. You called him Nice-Boy.

VIV. I didn't!

TOM. You did!

VIV. I –

TOM. I knew it.

VIV. Alright.

TOM. I bloody knew it.

VIV. Okay.

TOM. Caught you red-handed!

VIV. Oh, fuck off.

TOM. Ha.

I love it when you swear. It's sexy.

VIV. Is it?

TOM. Very sexy.

VIV. Hmmm. What time is their train getting in?

TOM. Oh no, don't change the subject.

VIV. I'm not – I just want to know if we've got enough time before they get here.

TOM. For what?

VIV. . . .

What time is their train getting in?

TOM. She said it was one – one –

She said it was one –

. . .

VIV. **Tom?**

TOM. Hmm? Yes?

VIV. What time does it say on this clock?

TOM. Sorry I was – was –

VIV. That's okay. What time does it say?

TOM. It's erm – erm – Sorry, I was never much one for – time-keeping, you know?

VIV. That's alright.

TOM. Always – Er, it's erm – It's one – one-thirty.

VIV. **Two-thirty.**

TOM. Two-thirty.

VIV. You said you'd be home early tonight.

TOM. I know, sorry, yeah, we – Rehearsals ran over then we – Had to run straight over to the club,

Marco had some people he wanted us to meet – So –

VIV. How was Marco?

TOM. Same as ever. He says hi.

VIV. He listen to the demo?

TOM. He did.

VIV. And?

TOM. He likes it.

VIV. What does that mean?

TOM. It means he likes it.

Have you been waiting up?

VIV. Alice woke me. Couldn't sleep so I sat up with her.

TOM. She asleep now?

VIV. Yes.

TOM. I'll have a look in.

VIV. Don't. She's –

TOM. It's okay. I'll just –

VIV. Don't. I only just got her off.

TOM. Okay. Just I haven't seen her all day –

VIV. Well, that's what happens when you get in at three in the morning.

TOM. It was two-thirty a minute ago.

VIV. I rounded up.

TOM. …

How was – How was your day?

VIV. Fine. Jenny called.

TOM. Did she?

VIV. Wanted to know if I'd had any more thoughts about the job. Said I was still talking to you about it.

She was asking after you.

TOM. Jenny?

VIV. Alice.

She asked me if I knew where you went every night.

TOM. Viv –

VIV. Said I didn't know. I just said 'Out.'

TOM. Would you stop –

VIV. What?

TOM. It's two in the morning, I'm just –

VIV. Two-thirty –

TOM. I don't have the energy to argue with –

VIV. Have the energy to go out drinking till two-thirty.

TOM. Would you stop it with the time? Because I am fully aware that is two thirty and I am tired and worn out and now I'm shouting and I'm going to wake up –

. . .

Jesus.

Christ.

When did you become such a miserable bitch?

VIV. I don't know, Tom. When did you stop giving me a reason to smile?

TOM. **You're always smiling.**

VIV. I can't help it – I'm a smiley person.

TOM. And here was me thinking I made you smile.

VIV. Oh no, it's everything, the – The music, the drink, the dancing –

TOM. I could dance with you all night.

VIV. All night?

TOM. Well I couldn't just dance with you once, could I? You'd be devastated.

VIV. Would I?

TOM. Oh absolutely. In fact, now I've started, I don't think I can ever really stop without upsetting you, and as a gentleman I would never dream of upsetting a lady.

VIV. How noble of you.

TOM. Oh, you're too kind, Viv.

VIV. Who's Viv?

TOM. I – Oh my God, I am – Sorry, I'm so – My brain is – The old noggin's not the greatest at the best of times –

VIV. A gentleman would never forget a lady's name.

TOM. Oh, I never said I was a gentleman.

VIV. You just said it now.

TOM. No, no you must have misheard me. I could never be a gentleman.

VIV. No?

…

Oh. Oh no. You are definitely not a gentleman. A gentleman would never kiss like that.

What else would a gentleman definitely not do?

TOM. Wouldn't you like to know?

VIV. Yes. I would.

TOM. Let me show you, Viv.

VIV. Viv again.

TOM. Fuck, sorry I –

VIV. Who is she?

TOM. No one, she –

VIV. **Who is she?**

Who is she?

TOM. It's not –

VIV. What was her name?

TOM. I –

I don't know.

VIV. …

When?

TOM. A few weeks back.

VIV. Was she the only one?

TOM. Yes.

Yes, I swear, she was the only –

VIV. How many times did you –

TOM. Twice. Once that night and again a week later.

VIV. Where?

TOM. We met at the club, and then we – at her place.

VIV. What was it like?

TOM. . . .

VIV. What was it like?

TOM. It was – I –

. . .

VIV. . . .

TOM. I'm so sorry, Viv. I'm so –

. . .

Ow. Okay. Okay I –

. . .

Okay – Ow! Ow, stop it Viv, stop –

VIV. Fucking –

TOM. Stop – Come on, Viv, come on –

VIV. – bastard, you fucking fucking –

TOM. Viv! Viv! Come on. Come on. Stop hitting –

VIV. Fucking – bastard. Fucking –

TOM. Stop it!

VIV. Get off me!

TOM. Viv, stop –

VIV. Get off –

TOM. **Hey come on, come on – it's okay. It's okay –**

VIV. It's not.

TOM. It's okay, darling, everything's gonna be –

VIV. It's not okay!

TOM. Okay, okay.

VIV. It's not – He's such a fucking –

TOM. I know.

VIV. – fucking –

TOM. What did he say, darling? What did Russell –

VIV. He didn't say anything!

TOM. What, nothing?

VIV. He didn't say anything, he just said that – I'd picked him up from the airport, and I was really excited to see him, telling him about all the things I'd got planned –

TOM. Right.

VIV. – but he didn't seem that – excited, he just – Kept talking about how tired he was from exams and this term and – how difficult it was for him us being apart –

TOM. Right –

VIV. – and it's been hard for me too, I said that but – Then he said he'd been thinking about college and us and long distance and he didn't know if it was right for him now, if we were right together right now. If this was right for us – And I said, What do you mean you don't know if we're – if we're – And now we're having this huge fucking argument and I've only just picked him up from the airport!

TOM. Okay, okay, okay –

VIV. I don't know what to do!

TOM. It's fine.

VIV. How is this fine? How is anything about this fine, how could anything possibly be –

TOM. Alright, I –

VIV. You keep – saying it's going to be okay but it's not!

TOM. Of course it is! Of course it's going to be okay!

VIV. How do you know?

TOM. Because.

VIV. Because what?

TOM. Because you don't think – you don't think things like this don't happen all the time to people? You don't think this sort of thing didn't happen to your mother and me?

VIV. It did?

TOM. Of course! We – What d'you think we – I mean, just cos you love someone doesn't mean you're gonna love them – all the time. In fact sometimes it's going to be really bloody hard. But if you love each other you get through it, you work through it and it makes you better cos of it so –

It'll be okay.

Come here.

Better?

Gives us a smile. You look serious. Very serious. And red. And puffy.

VIV. Alright.

TOM. Like a tomato.

VIV. Fuck off.

TOM. Like a big, serious tomato. You look awful.

VIV. Fuck off – you look awful.

TOM. No, you do.

VIV. You do. **Christ, you look awful.**

TOM. Thanks. Can I come in?

VIV. Sure.

TOM. . . .

Funny being back. Still looks the same.

VIV. Why wouldn't it?

TOM. I don't – I mean, it's only been – but I –

. . .

VIV. Where have you been staying?

TOM. Stefan put me up. On his sofa, so that's –

VIV. Right.

TOM. Where's Alice?

VIV. She's playing with a friend.

TOM. She not here then?

VIV. No.

TOM. Right. Right, it's just I thought –

VIV. What?

TOM. Well, I haven't seen her for two weeks, I wanted to –

VIV. What?

TOM. I thought – I thought maybe she'd be here, I could see her –

VIV. Well, she's playing with a friend so – I thought best if she wasn't here for now.

TOM. When can I see her?

VIV. I don't know.

TOM. How is she?

VIV. She's good.

TOM. She miss me?

VIV. Yes.

TOM. Do you miss me?

VIV. . . .

I took the job. Gave my notice. Putting the flat on the market, some stuff's going to go into haulage, rest we'll sell and – Wanted to tell you to your face, so –

TOM. Viv –

VIV. Starts next term but I want to head back a bit early, look at schools for Alice –

TOM. Viv, you can't.

VIV. Why not?

TOM. We haven't even – talked about this –

VIV. We don't have anything to talk about.

TOM. We do, we do, Viv, we –

VIV. Tom, we don't –

TOM. We fucking do!

VIV. No, we don't.

TOM. I miss you, Viv.

VIV. Don't – Just –

TOM. I miss you. And Alice –

VIV. Don't you fucking –

TOM. I miss you! I fucking – I miss you so much I'm sick. I'm sick. I'm sick of living out of a suitcase and sleeping on Stefan's fucking sofa and not being able to speak to anyone in the same fucking – I can't sleep. I can't think, my mind's a – mess, I can't think straight, my head's all – I can't play any more. My hands are like – that – on the keys. I'm fucked and I've fucked up and I'm sorry and I need you to forgive me cos if you go and leave me here then I am well and truly fucked cos I won't have a home any more. I could wander this whole miserable fucking planet from top to bottom and I wouldn't find anywhere cos I wouldn't have you. This, this is my – You and me and us and Alice. You're my home.

…

Can I come home?

Please?

VIV.…

TOM.…

…

Okay.

Okay.

I'll just –

VIV. Don't –

TOM.…

VIV. Don't – Don't go.

…

TOM.…

Okay.

Okay.

Viv –

VIV. Tom, don't –

TOM. No, I need to –

VIV. Please –

TOM. Viv, I just – you don't have to say anything or promise me anything now but I just need to know – Are we going to be okay?

Am I going to be okay?

VIV. It's like plaque.

TOM. Plaque? Like – your teeth plaque?

VIV. Yes. You get clumps of it growing across the cells, blocking the pathways and signals. And the cells – this is perhaps a little –

TOM. Just – please.

VIV. The cells are supposed to be straight – like that – so they don't collide with each other. But they start to break down and get tangled and collapse, the messages to the brain get mixed up, wires get crossed which means they can't carry all the things the cells need any more so they die.

TOM. And what – what causes it?

VIV. No one's exactly sure. There are lots of theories – diet, genetics – but no one is totally certain.

TOM. So what happens next?

VIV. Well, we start you on a course of –

TOM. No, I mean to me. What happens to me next?

VIV. Well – it's difficult to say exactly. Each case is unique and the steps – it's not possible to say exactly how quickly – Many people have gone on for years leading very healthy, normal lives before they need to consider –

TOM. Just – tell me exactly what the next step is.

VIV. It's not as simple as that. It's not as simple as this step then that step. You know? One step, two step.

One step, two step.

One step, two step.

TOM. One step –

VIV. – two step.

TOM. Legs loose –

VIV. – but strong. Back straight –

TOM. – nice and long.

VIV. Very nice.

TOM. Un pas, deux pas.

VIV. *Oh très bien!*

TOM. *Merci.*

VIV. *De rien.*

TOM. Can I call you?

VIV. Call me what?

TOM. Alice.

VIV. Alice?

TOM. Yeah.

VIV. I like it.

TOM. Alice.

VIV. Again, Daddy, again!

TOM. Okay, okay. Round and round the garden, like a teddy bear.

VIV. One step –

TOM. Two step –

VIV. Three years.

TOM. She'll be back before you know it.

VIV. I know.

TOM. You'll just have to do with me till then.

VIV. Then what?

TOM. That finger – and then that finger on that key and then –

VIV. Oh God.

TOM. No, no you're doing it, just – There. That's a G.

VIV. How do you do it?

TOM. Easy. Here, you give it a try.

VIV. I can't.

TOM. You're thinking too much –

VIV. Oh my God, I –

TOM. Try again. One, two, three. Easy. One, two, three. Like dancing. One step, two step.

VIV. One step, two step.

Round and round the garden like a teddy bear, one step, two step tickly under there!

Tickly under there!

Tickly under there.

Garden looks alright, doesn't it? Be beautiful in spring. Nurse says they get all sorts. Foxgloves and poppies and Busy Lizzies and forget-me-nots.

Alice sends her love. And Russell and the boys. You should see them, Jesus they're like tanks, they're huge. I keep saying it's cos of the big portions they serve over there. She sent me some photos from when they went to visit Russell's parents in Florida. You could barely see them over the top of their food, they were like – huge mountains of –

Doctors say you haven't been eating properly. Say you won't touch your food. Why you not eating, Tom? Hmmm? Why you not eating? You don't like it? You not hungry? They say you've been quiet. Moody too. Haven't been getting up to your usual – Stopped listening to your music and –

Say something, Tom. For me, eh? You were real chatty when I last came to see you. Real chatterbox. Couldn't stop then, couldn't stop you from – Oh, Tom, your hands are like ice! Why didn't you – Why aren't you wearing your sweater? I packed you your blue – I put in your – where is it? Where is it, I'm sure put it in the – God, I must've – Forgotten to pack it in all – thing – of the move. Swear I put it in your bag. Christ, I'm the one who's losing it now, I – There. There, come here, Tom. Tom, come here.

TOM. No.

VIV. Come here.

TOM. No ca-can't-ca–

VIV. Tom, just

TOM. Can't can't can't!

VIV. Tom, just –

TOM. Aaaaah!

VIV. Tom!

TOM. Aaaaah!

VIV. Tom please, for the love of God, just –

TOM. Don't!

VIV. Just put your –

TOM. No!

VIV. Just put your hand in the sleeve –

TOM. Bitch.

VIV. Ow!

TOM. Bitch!

VIV. Tom, you're hurting me.

TOM. Fucking –

VIV. Tom, you are hurting me – get off! Get off!

TOM. Fucking – fuck fuck b-b-bi-bi–

VIV. Jesus, Tom, let go of me! Let go of me! Let go, let –

You hurt me, Tom, just now. You hurt me.

TOM. You hurt me.

VIV. I don't like it.

TOM. Neither do I. Why do you do it?

VIV. I don't – I don't do anything, Tom.

TOM. Well, I don't do it either.

VIV. I'm not doing anything, Tom! I'm just – to put your jumper on, I –

You understand? I'm just trying to –

You don't know how strong your grip is. It's like iron round me. You don't know, Tom, you don't –

Why do you do it, Tom? Why do you –

Well, say something! Say something, you – you – Don't just sit there drooling at me like some – some – like some pig-eyed sack of shit, say something! Tom. Anything, please just – just –

I don't know what to do, Tom. I don't know what to do with you. And I don't know what to do without you. I – I – You used to look at me and it made me melt you loved me so much but now it's – nothing. If I keep coming here, Tom, there's going be nothing of me left. I'll be as empty as you are and pretty soon it'll just be the two of us sitting here, two dribbling idiots just waiting for someone to come round to turn the lights out.

I can't do this any more, Tom. I can't – I can't – I'm not –

I'm sorry, Tom. I'm so, so – I tried. I really, really tried.

…

…

Okay.

Okay.

Okay.

Tom, let go. Let go, Tom, let –

TOM. I da-da–

VIV. Tom, please, please let –

TOM. Watu b-b-b–

VIV. Tom!

TOM. Wat to – no! No!

VIV. **Tommy! Let go of my –**

TOM. No! No!

VIV. Tommy, for Christ's sake let go of me, I swear you are –

TOM. I – I –

VIV. Oh my God.

TOM. I – I –

VIV. Oh my God, you – Oh Jesus, Tommy! Jesus, it's all over you! You stupid little –

TOM. I'm sorry!

VIV. What is wrong with –

TOM. I'm sorry!

VIV. You test my patience, Tommy, you really do.

TOM. I didn't mean it!

VIV. Are you a baby? Are you a stupid little baby? Are you a big boy or are you a stupid little baby who pisses himself like a –

TOM. I'm sor–

VIV. Stop saying that!

TOM. Aaaah!

VIV. Don't you start –

TOM. Waaaah!

VIV. Come on, get out of these –

TOM. Waaaah!

VIV. Stop it!

TOM. No.

VIV. You stop it now, do you hear me or you'll get a smack, you understand?

TOM. No!

VIV. Come here!

TOM. No!

VIV. Come here you little – !

. . .

. . .

. . .

Oh my God, Tommy, I – I'm so sorry, I am so –

I didn't mean to hit you. I didn't mean to – I didn't mean to shout at you, Tommy, it's just I – Mummy lost her temper for a minute, she didn't think what she was doing. Mummy would never hurt you. Did I hurt you?

TOM. Mm-hm.

VIV. Where? Show Mummy where.

TOM. Here.

VIV. There? Just there? On your leg.

TOM. And here.

VIV. Is that sore?

TOM. Yes.

VIV. Should I kiss it better? Would you like Mummy to kiss it better?

TOM. . . .

VIV. There. Does that feel better?

TOM. A little.

VIV. How about that? Is that better?

TOM. Yes.

VIV. Shall we take these off and wash them? Shall we get these smelly old things off?

TOM. Okay.

VIV. Get you nice and clean. Make you feel nicer.

TOM. Okay.

VIV. There you go. Get your little button and your zipper. Let me get these off.

There. Does that feel better?

TOM. I – I –

VIV. Doesn't that feel better?

TOM. I'm not –

VIV. Does that feel good?

TOM. Don't –

VIV. Shall I kiss it better?

TOM. Viv –

VIV. You want me to kiss it better?

TOM. Viv, I –

VIV. Let me kiss it. Let me kiss it.

TOM. Stop –

VIV. Let me feel it, let me feel –

TOM. Stop it! Stop it, Viv, stop it just stop it!

VIV. . . .

I'm sorry, I'm sorry, I – I –

Was it not – nice?

TOM. No it's –

VIV. Was I not doing it right?

TOM. No, it's –

VIV. What d'you want me to do? Tell me what – feels good and I'll –

TOM. It's not – stop it, would you? Just stop it, just – Leave it, it doesn't matter, it's not –

. . .

VIV. . . .

What's wrong? Is it the drugs?

TOM. Leave it, will you?

VIV. Dr Martin said they might affect your –

TOM. Just leave it!

VIV. Okay. Okay.

. . .

TOM. Don't –

VIV. Where you going? Come here, I don't wanna – I just wanna cuddle is all, I don't wanna – do anything else.

VIV *sings the first verse of 'The Way You Look Tonight'.*

TOM. . . .

What will you do, Viv?

VIV. What do you mean?

TOM. What will you do – when it gets worse?

VIV. What do you think I'll do?

TOM. . . .

VIV *sings the second verse of 'The Way You Look Tonight'.* TOM *and* VIV *sing the third verse. They alternate lines and share the final line of the verse.*

Keep that breathless – keep that breathless – less –

Keep that – that – keep that –

VIV. *Keep that breathless charm –*

TOM. *Keep that breathless cha– cha–Keep that b-b-b–*

VIV. *Keep that breathless ch–*

TOM. *Keep that b-b-b-breathless cha- ch-ch-ch-cha-charm –*
Keep that breathless ch-ch-charm
Wo – Wo – W-w-won't you p-p-pplease – please –

Please. Please.

Won't you pleeeease arraaaange-ge-ge –range it 'cause
I love you – love you – love –

Just the way you –

Just the way you –

You –

You –

Just the way you –

End.